Best kept secrets of

POWER

AND

PERSUASION

BY

Randolph Britain

TABLE OF CONTENTS

PRE-INTRODUCTION

Before you read any further, I must warn you that the contents of this book are not for the faint hearted. It's highly likely that the information found here will change your world view forever. But if you're ready for that, read on.

If you're like me, you've probably read numerous books that have four and five-star reviews but fail to deliver what they promise in their promotional hype. Often, such books just drag information out over 300 pages that could have easily been delivered in 30 or less. Sadly, some books don't even deliver at all!

It's that kind of experience that inspired the structure of this book, a book that has been specifically designed to deliver its valuable information quickly and efficiently, without pages and pages of unnecessary filler. Book snobs may decry it, critics may attack it, but if I've done my job right, you'll love it!

INTRODUCTION

To Manipulate means

"To control or influence a person cleverly or unscrupulously."

Do you know when you're being manipulated, or are you oblivious to it all? Well, let's find out by asking one simple question.

Can you recognize and name the two ultra- powerful formulas applied to the title of this book?

If you can answer that question correctly, you are well informed and protected. If you can't, you need this book. That's because without the information found here, you're not seeing the techniques that make you vulnerable to manipulation and place you at a significant disadvantage to a privileged few who use the techniques every day, to their advantage and to your detriment!

When I discovered that my own family and friends were in that position, I set to work writing this book. I wrote it to protect them from manipulation. I published it to help you do the same.

Don't live the rest of your life at a disadvantage to others, instead, read this book now and discover what the privileged few don't want you to know.

Remember, knowledge is power and forewarned is forearmed!

POWERFUL, PERSUASIVE,
MEMORABLE

A s a child, you were probably told the story of Little Red Riding Hood or The Wolf in Sheep's Clothing. Perhaps you were told both. Such stories or versions of them are told to children all over the world at a very young age.

This is done to instill the fundamentally important life lessons that you can't always trust something that looks warm and friendly, and you must always be on the lookout for hidden danger.

But spotting hidden danger is easier said than done, especially so if you don't know what you're looking for in the first place. That's precisely what happened when you looked at the title of this book. You didn't (and still don't) see the wolf in sheep's clothing hiding in plain sight, because you don't possess the necessary knowledge to do that. Essentially, you were completely defenseless to my deliberate attempt to seduce, attract and persuade you to choose this book above all others. If you've come this far, then the formula has worked as planned. Once you know and understand that formula you, too, will be able to harness the power of the techniques by duplicating them yourself. So, without further ado, let's get to the crux of the matter!

When you look at the title of this book you are looking at two of the most powerful formulas known to man. The first one we will concentrate on is called a Tricolon, and it's been used to seduce, attract, and persuade people just like you and me for over two thousand years. Yes, you did read that correctly and it's quite a revelation if you weren't aware of it. For most of your life you have been seduced, attracted, and sometimes manipulated by a two and a half thousand-year-old persuasive technique and never known it! And don't be put off by the Tricolon's fancy Greek name. A Tricolon is just three words, sentences or phrases combined to give a single powerful impression. 'Friends, Romans Countryman', 'I'm Lovin it' and 'Drain the Swamp' are just three classic examples of the Tricolon formula that you may already be familiar with.

I must make something clear here from the outset. We are not talking about the random or haphazard use of the formula we have all used at some point. We're talking about the strategic and deliberate use of it to seduce, attract and persuade a target audience.

It probably won't come as any surprise that politicians across the entire political spectrum deliberately use the Tricolon formula to manipulate their target audience. I wasn't surprised by that either. But what did surprise me was that Julius Caesar, William Shakespeare, Jane Austen, Charles Dickens and others deliberately applied it to manipulate their target audience!

When I say manipulate, I am referring to the dictionary definition as in, 'controlling or influencing a person cleverly or unscrupulously'. As we continue you will see the many further examples of the Tricolon formula at work (in its three major formats), and I will leave it to you to decide whether it was or is used in an unscrupulous manner.

I think most of us understand and, to some extent, expect politicians to use all manner of cunning and creative methods to seduce, attract and persuade their target audience. Some might say almost anything is justified in order to win your vote and get into power, at least that's how it often seems. But I think a lot of people would be surprised to discover that Jane Austen and William Shakespeare used the exact same tactics and formulas as Barak Obama, Donald Trump, Joe Biden, etc. to seduce their target audience. It certainly surprised me!

I certainly never perceived William Shakespeare, Jane Austen, and Charles Dickens as manipulative. Perhaps, naively, I thought their words just naturally flowed onto the page to stir the mind and soul of the reader. Turns out they used every trick in the book to reel us in.

As soon as I realized this, I must admit that I felt a bit conned and taken advantage of. I wondered why on earth this was not common knowledge.

I, for one, like to know when I'm being deliberately manipulated. I think most of us feel the same way, so I set out on a mission to learn more so I could inform my children and make them aware of the techniques. Hopefully then they could see through them. This is particularly important when the techniques are being used unscrupulously.

Later, we'll look more closely at why the information might not be common knowledge, but for now, take a moment to process your thoughts and allow the eye-opening information you just learned to sink in.

If you chose to download and read this book you probably just learned for the first time that William Shakespeare, Donald Trump, Jane Austen, McDonalds, Nike, KFC and many others have something in common in the way they all deliberately set out to manipulate you using the exact same techniques. They all used the same two and a half thousand-year-old persuasive technique called a Tricolon.

If you're feeling a bit skeptical right now, it's completely understandable. But hang in there, I'm going to show you numerous examples of the Tricolon formula at work.

The Coca Cola slogan, **Taste the Feeling**, is the deliberate application of the Tricolon formula, as is McDonald's **I'm Lovin' It**, KFC's **Finger Lickin' Good**, Nike's **Just Do It** and Adidas's **Impossible is Nothing**, and so on. The formula might be two and a half thousand years old, but it works as well now as it did then. This is exactly why it's the go-to formula for all the global companies above. Now that you know and can recognize the basic three-word Tricolon formula, you will see it everywhere. Now that you have the knowledge you can see the Wolf in Sheep's Clothing hiding in plain sight. Congratulations, and welcome to the land of the well informed and privileged few.

Politicians and advertising agencies use the formula extensively because of its reliability. Just spend 30 minutes watching a TV channel, for example, and you'll see the tricolon everywhere. Fox news in the USA is a great example. Checkout some of their Tricolon usage below:

"Fox & Friends" "Fox News Alert" "Forbes on Fox" "Fox News Watch" "Fox News Sunday" "Fox Means Business" "Fox News Live", "Sheppard Smith Reporting", "Keep It Here", "Tucker Carlson Tonight", Packed and Stacked", "Fair and Balanced", "Sunday Morning Futures", "Wherever You Go".

Of course, we've all used the formula haphazardly or by accident. It's all around us every day and as a result we all pick it up loosely through a process of cultural osmosis. But only a privileged few in society are actually taught the real power of the formula, and when and how to use it most effectively. Again, I reiterate: the strategic and deliberate use of the formula is the key.

As I stated earlier, the concept of the tricolon is over two thousand years old and it was first identified in Ancient Greece. We'll look at what we know about the history of it in a later chapter, but the word itself is derived from two Greek words, tria, meaning 'three' and Kolon meaning 'member' or 'clause'.

Today you will often hear it referred to as a triad, the rule of three, or the power of three, all of which basically describe the same tricolon formula.

One of the oldest and most famous recorded examples of the Tricolon comes from Julius Caesars's letter to the Roman Senate in 47BC. He used the ascending Tricolon, 'Veni, Vidi, Vici' to describe the swift and conclusive victory he had achieved in one of his many battles. Translated, this means, "I came, I saw, I conquered!" This is technically known as an ascending Tricolon with Anaphora, which means the phrase comes in three parts, in ascending order, with the final part delivered in a forceful crescendo at the end. In this example, "I conquered!"

At the time Caesar applied it the formula was just a couple of hundred years old, but Caesar was from the ruling classes so he had received the best education with a great emphasis on the study of rhetoric and the art of persuasion. He certainly knew how to put a memorable phrase together, and we're still talking about it and remembering it more than two thousand years later.

Let's look at some further examples of the basic three-word formula tricolon that you might be familiar with:

"Keep America Great", "Build the Wall", "I'll Be Back", "Lock Her Up", "Where's The Beef?", "Impossible is Nothing",

"Vorsprung durch Technik", 'Build Back Better', "Read My Lips", "Run Hide Fight", "Plead The Fifth", "Get Rich Quick", "Ban The Bomb", "Taste The Feeling", "Just Do It", "Finger Licking Good", "Go Fund Me", "Peace Through Strength", "Vote For Change", "Brexit Means Brexit", "Repeal and Replace" "Yes We Can", "Every Little Helps", "Fighting For Us", "Black Lives Matter" "White Lives Matter", "Believe In Better", "Education, Education, Education", "Follow The Money", "Whip Inflation Now", "I Like Ike", "Imagination At Work", "Save Our Souls", "Je suis Charlie", "Armed and Ready", "Suited and Booted" "Hope and Glory" "Bring It On", "Back In Black", Make Today Special", "Spiritually, Ecumenically, Grammatically".

"Pride and Prejudice", "The Great Gatsby", "War and Peace", "Best Kept Secret", "Bravo Two Zero", "Fifty Shades Darker", "Cometh The Hour", "The Pelican Brief", "First Among Equals", "Paths of Glory", "The Secret Pilgrim", "Honour Among Thieves", "The Perfect Spy", "In Cold Blood", "A Delicate Truth", "The Night Manager", "Twelve Red Herrings", "The Last Juror", "The New Enemy", "Sleepless in Seattle", "Bridge of Spies", "Saving Private Ryan", "The Big Short", "The Hunger Games", "Million Dollar Baby", "Saturday Night Fever", "Diamonds are Forever", "My Fair Lady", "Gentlemen Prefer

Blondes", "The French Connection", "Beverley Hills Cop", "Last Action Hero", "Leaving Las Vegas", "Walk The Line", "Stand By Me", "The Shawshank Redemption", "Good Will Hunting", "The Full Monty", "Field Of Dreams", "Enter The Dragon", "National Lampoons Vacation", "The Deer Hunter", "Behind Enemy Lines", "Alice in Wonderland", "Quantum of Solace", "The Italian Job", "End Of Days".

"Game of Thrones", "The West Wing", "Strictly Come Dancing", "Britain's Got Talent", "The One Show", "Good Morning Britain", "Good Morning America", "House Of Cards", "The Twilight Zone", "Crime Scene Investigation", "Everybody Loves Raymond", "The Big Questions", "The Vampire Diaries", "Hill Street Blues", "The Golden Girls", "The Rockford Files", "The Muppet Show", "Location, Location, Location", "Ramsey's Kitchen Nightmares", "Take Me Out", "Air Crash Investigation", "Britain's Got Talent", "America's Got Talent", "Keep Britain Tidy", "Battle Of Britain", "Forewarned Is Forearmed", "Kindle Paper White", "Kindle Direct Publishing", British Broadcasting Company (BBC), American Broadcasting Company (ABC), Cable Network News (CNN), National Broadcasting Company, Columbia Broadcasting System (CBS), Public Broadcasting Service, Quality Value Convenience (QVC), Imperial Chemical

Industries (ICI), Bavarian Motor Works (BMW), National Health Service (NHS), National Rifle Association (NRA), British Medical Association (BMA), Central Investigation Agency (CIA), Crown Prosecution Service (CPS), World Health Organization (WHO).

So, there you have it. The Tricolon formula is the formula of choice for Julius Caesar, Charles Dickens, Jane Austen, Barak Obama, Donald Trump, Winston Churchill, Jeffrey Archer, John Grisham, F. Scott Fitzgerald, John Le Carre', Steven Spielberg, Nike, Tesco, BMW, Audi, McDonalds, Fox News and many, many more.

See how the formula grabs your attention and sears into your memory? Remember, if you want to communicate your message in the most memorable and effective manner, then the Tricolon should be your first-choice formula. Use it in your email headings, and use it wisely and strategically to seduce, attract, and persuade your target audience. By doing this you (just like Nike, McDonald's and William Shakespeare) will ensure that your message gets noticed and remembered and not ignored and forgotten.

THREE PHRASE EXAMPLES

As we have seen, you don't have to stick to just three words. The Tricolon formula can be three phrases. Below are some examples of that:

I came, I saw, I conquered.

Lies, damn lies, and statistics.

The father, the son, and the Holy Spirit.

It's a bird! ...it's a plane! ...it's Superman!

Government of the people, by the people, for the people.

America is strong, America is proud, and America is free.

Thank you, God bless you, and God bless America.

THREE SENTENCE
EXAMPLES

A nd here are some 'three sentence examples' of the Tricolon:

Been there. Done that. Bought the T-shirt.

Find it. Get it. Argos it.

Tell me and I forget. Teach me and I remember. Involve me and I learn.

Freedom leads to prosperity. Freedom replaces the ancient hatreds among nations with comity and peace. Freedom is the victor.

The tricolon is something that you can use in your emails, reports, resumes, CV's, speeches, presentations, and your everyday conversations.

This is the practical application for you. I personally use the techniques in my email headings and reports, especially if I want something to be succinct, attractive, and memorable to the recipient.

Imagine how effective it can be when used in a CV submitted to a prospective employer. After skimming through your application, they won't realize exactly what it is that was attractive about the resume, but they will know they like it and they will remember it.

So, if you were one of the Little Red Riding Hood majority who had no idea about the existence of this ancient rhetorical device called a Tricolon, then welcome to the land of the well informed and protected. Welcome to the land of the privileged few.

WHERE IT BEGAN

T he discovery of the tricolon formula cannot be attributed to anyone person, but as of now, the oldest reliable evidence takes us back two thousand five hundred years to Syracuse on the Mediterranean island of Sicily.

Today Syracuse is a popular tourist destination, but back then, it was at the heart of the Ancient Greek Empire. Due to its strategic position, Syracuse grew rapidly and became one of the major cities that controlled the entire Mediterranean. By the 5th century AD, Syracuse had grown to become roughly the same size (in land mass and population) as Athens. Syracuse was a prominent cultural center that in later years became the birthplace of the legendary mathematician and engineer Archimedes.

But back in 465 BC Syracuse was governed by a rather unsavory character called Thrasybulus who was the last in a long line of tyrant rulers. Thrasybulus was thrown out of office after less than one year but, after his departure, life in Syracuse descended into chaos. This culminated in bitter feuds and battles amongst the population over land and other property rights.

During this chaotic period a man we know only as Corax came into prominence. Very little is known or recorded about Corax, but there is evidence of him through the writings of later historical figures such as Plato, Aristotle, and Cicero. As a result of Corax's persuasive skills, it is said that a state of order was eventually restored to Syracuse.

Exactly where Corax developed his unmatched negotiating and persuasive skills is uncertain, but it is believed that earlier in his life he may have been a courtier to Hieron, one of the previous tyrant rulers of Syracuse.

As previously stated, any accounts that still survive in relation to Corax come primarily from later writers, such as Plato, Aristotle and Cicero, but they do tend to support the case that Corax was one of the first people in the ancient world to set down the precepts of persuasive Greek rhetoric which includes the tricolon formula.

Corax is also credited with teaching other people his negotiating and persuasive skills and showing them how they could best open a speech and advance an everyday argument to achieve victory.

Newly discovered rhetorical formulas like the tricolon were further developed over time by notable figures such as Aristotle, Isocrates and Plato, and were quickly taken up and used by those in power as you can see from Caesar's famous 'Veni, Vidi, Veci' in 47BC.

YES WE CAN!

As we have seen, there is far more to the tricolon than just three words, and marketing agencies and politicians across the globe are fully aware of that. Whether it was Julius Caesar with "I came, I saw, I conquered" in 47 BC or Donald Trump with "Drain the Swamp" two thousand years later, the Tricolon has consistently been the most reliable method of creating a memorable sound bite.

But no president or world leader can do it alone, and none of them would be half as persuasive or convincing without a senior speech writer or, these days, an entire team dedicated to that cause. For John F. Kennedy it was Ted Sorenson. For Barak Obama it was John Favreau, for Donald Trump it was Stephen Miller. These people, and their teams, work tirelessly behind the scenes to help write some of the most memorable words to ever be uttered in history.

Let us look at how they do that by taking a peek behind the curtain at a speech by Barak Obama from November 4th, 2008. Obama delivered the speech to an audience of 240,000 people in

Grant Park, Chicago, Illinois as well as a global audience of many millions worldwide. It has become famous for one basic three-word Tricolon;

"Yes We Can!"

With your newly acquired knowledge, you will see that Barak Obama and John Favreau purposely chose to use the Tricolon more than twenty times in this speech, and not just with the "Yes We Can" phrase! I've highlighted the Tricolon usage in **bold** to reveal the wolf in sheep's clothing stealthily lying-in wait. Ready to seduce its prey. Below is the speech in its entirety.

"If there is anyone out there **who still doubts** that America is a place where all things are possible; **who still wonders** if the dream of our founders is alive in our time; **who still questions** the power of our democracy, tonight is your answer.

It's the answer told by lines that stretched around schools and churches in numbers this nation has never seen; by people who waited three hours and four hours, many for the very first time in their lives, because they believed that this time must be different; that their voices could be that difference.

It's the answer spoken by young and old, rich and poor, Democrat and Republican, black, white, Hispanic, Asian, Native American, gay, straight, disabled and not disabled - Americans who sent a message to the world that we have never been just a collection of individuals or a collection of Red States and Blue States: **we are, and always will be, the United States of America.**

It's the answer that led those who have been told for so long by so many to be cynical, and fearful, and doubtful of what we can achieve to put their hands on the arc of history and bend it once more toward the hope of a better day.

It's been a long time coming, but tonight, because of what we did **on this day, in this election, at this defining moment**, change has come to America.

A little bit earlier this evening I received an extraordinarily gracious call from Senator McCain. He fought long and hard in this campaign, and he's fought even longer and harder for the country he loves. He has endured sacrifices for America that most of us cannot begin to imagine. We are better off for the service rendered by this brave and selfless leader.

I congratulate him, I congratulate Governor Palin, for all they have achieved, **and I look forward to working with them** to renew this nation's promise in the months ahead.

I want to thank my partner in this journey, a man who campaigned from his heart and spoke for the men and women he grew up with on the streets of Scranton and rode with on that train home to Delaware, the vice-president-elect of the United States, Joe Biden.

And I would not be standing here tonight without the unyielding support of **my best friend** for the last 16 years, **the rock of our family, the love of my life**, the nation's next first lady, Michelle Obama. Sasha and Malia, I love you both more than you can imagine, and you have earned the new puppy that's coming with us to the White House.

And while she's no longer with us, I know my grandmother is watching, along with the family that made me who I am. I miss them tonight, and know that my debt to them is beyond measure. To my sister Maya, my sister Auma, all my other brothers and sisters - thank you so much for all the support you have given me. I am grateful to them.

To my campaign manager David Plouffe, the unsung hero of this campaign, who built the best political campaign in the history of the United States of America. My chief strategist David Axelrod, who has been a partner with me every step of the way, and to the best campaign team ever assembled in the history of politics - you made this happen, and I am forever grateful for what you've sacrificed to get it done.

But above all, I will never forget who this victory truly belongs to - it belongs to you.

I was never the likeliest candidate for this office. We didn't start with much money or many endorsements. Our campaign was not hatched in the halls of Washington - it began in the backyards of Des Moines and the living rooms of Concord and the front porches of Charleston.

It was built by working men and women who dug into what little savings they had to give $5 and $10 and $20 to the cause.

It grew strength from the young people who rejected the myth of their generation's apathy; who left their homes and their families for jobs that offered little pay and less sleep; it grew strength from the not-so-young people who braved the bitter cold and scorching heat to knock on the doors of perfect strangers; from the millions of Americans who volunteered, and organized, and proved that more than two centuries later, **a government of the people, by the people and for the people** has not perished from the Earth.

This is your victory.

I know you didn't do this just to win an election and I know you didn't do it for me. You did it because you understand the enormity of the task that lies ahead. For even as we celebrate tonight, we know the challenges that tomorrow will bring are the greatest of our lifetime - two wars, a planet in peril, the worst financial crisis in a century.

Even as we stand here tonight, we know there are brave Americans waking up in the deserts of Iraq and the mountains of Afghanistan to risk their lives for us.

There are mothers and fathers who will lie awake after their children fall asleep and wonder **how they'll make the mortgage, or pay their doctor's bills, or save enough for their child's college education**. There is new energy to harness and new jobs to be created; new schools to build and threats to meet and alliances to repair.

The road ahead will be long. Our climb will be steep. We may not get there in one year or even in one term, but America - I have never been more hopeful than I am tonight that we will get there. I promise you - we as a people will get there.

There will be setbacks and false starts. There are many who won't agree with every decision or policy I make as president, and we know that government can't solve every problem. But I will always be honest with you about the challenges we face. I will listen to you, especially when we disagree.

And above all, I will ask you to join in the work of remaking this nation the only way it's been done in America for 221 years - block by **block, brick by brick, calloused hand by calloused hand.**

What began 21 months ago in the depths of winter cannot end on this autumn night. This victory alone is not the change we seek - it is only the chance for us to make that change. And that cannot happen if we go back to the way things were. It cannot happen without you, without a new spirit of service, a new spirit of sacrifice.

So **let us summon** a new spirit of patriotism; of service and responsibility where each of us resolves to pitch in and work harder and look after not only ourselves, but each other. **Let us**

remember that if this financial crisis taught us anything, it's that we cannot have a thriving Wall Street while Main Street suffers - in this country, we rise or fall as one nation; as one people.

Let us resist the temptation to fall back on the same **partisanship and pettiness and immaturity** that has poisoned our politics for so long. Let us remember that it was a man from this state who first carried the banner of the Republican Party to the White House - a party founded on the values of **self-reliance, individual liberty, and national unity**.

Those are values that we all share, and while the Democratic Party has won a great victory tonight, we do so with a measure of humility and determination to heal the divides that have held back our progress. As Lincoln said to a nation far more divided than ours: "We are not enemies, but friends... though passion may have strained it must not break our bonds of affection."

And to those Americans whose support I have yet to earn - I may not have won your vote tonight, but **I hear your voices, I need your help, and I will be your president too.**

And to all those watching tonight from beyond our shores, from parliaments and palaces to those who are huddled around radios in the forgotten corners of the world - our stories are singular, but **our destiny is shared, and a new dawn of American leadership is at hand**.

To those who would tear the world down - we will defeat you. To those who seek peace and security - we support you.

And to all those who have wondered if America's beacon still burns as bright - tonight we proved once more that the true strength of our nation comes not from the might of our arms or the scale of our wealth, but from the enduring power of our ideals: democracy, liberty, opportunity and unyielding hope.

For that is the true genius of America - that America can change. Our union can be perfected. And what we have already achieved gives us hope for what we can and must achieve tomorrow.

This election had many firsts and many stories that will be told for generations. But one that's on my mind tonight is about a woman who cast her ballot in Atlanta. She's a lot like the millions of others who stood in line to make their voice heard in this election except for one thing - Ann Nixon Cooper is 106 years old.

She was born just a generation past slavery; a time when there were no cars on the road or planes in the sky; when someone like her couldn't vote for two reasons - because she was a woman and because of the color of her skin.

And tonight, I think about all that she's seen throughout her century in America - the heartache and the hope; the struggle and the progress; the times we were told that we can't, and the people who pressed on with that American creed: **Yes, we can**.

At a time when women's voices were silenced and their hopes dismissed, she lived to see them **stand up and speak out and reach for the ballot.**

Yes, we can.

When there was despair in the dust bowl and depression across the land, she saw a nation conquer fear itself with a **New Deal, new jobs and a new sense of common purpose. Yes, we can.**

When the bombs fell on our harbor and tyranny threatened the world, she was there to witness a generation rise to greatness and a democracy was saved. **Yes, we can.**

She was there for the buses in Montgomery, the hoses in Birmingham, a bridge in Selma, and a preacher from Atlanta who told a people that "we shall overcome". **Yes, we can.**

A man touched down on the Moon, a wall came down in Berlin, a world was connected by our own science and

imagination. And this year, in this election, she touched her finger to a screen, and cast her vote, because after 106 years in America, through the best of times and the darkest of hours, she knows how America can change. **Yes, we can.**

America, we have come so far. We have seen so much. But there is so much more to do. So tonight, let us ask ourselves - if our children should live to see the next century; if my daughters should be so lucky to live as long as Ann Nixon Cooper, what change will they see? What progress will we have made?

This is our chance to answer that call. **This is our moment**.

This is our time - to put our people back to work and open doors of opportunity for our kids; to restore prosperity and promote the cause of peace; to reclaim the American dream and reaffirm that fundamental truth - that out of many, we are one; that while we breathe, we hope, and where we are met with cynicism and doubt, and those who tell us that we can't, we will respond with that timeless creed that sums up the spirit of a people: **yes, we can.**

Thank you, God bless you, and may God bless the United States of America."

So, there you have it in clear written letters. The wolf in sheep's clothing reveals, and a master class in how to apply the Tricolon

31

formula in various forms to maximum effect. It certainly worked effectively for Barak Obama as we continue to speak about it today in the same way we still speak about Julius Caesar's 'Veni, Vidi, Vici' two thousand years later. Most people do not remember the two thousand and sixty-five words that made up Barak Obama's speech, but they do remember the basic three-word Tricolon "**Yes We Can**".

How you use the Tricolon formula is essentially up to you, but now you know how to use it. It can be as simple as "Drain the Swamp" or "Lock her Up" or as complex as a two-thousand-word speech, but if you use the Tricolon well, you will ensure that what you say gets noticed and remembered, and not ignored and forgotten.

FAVOURITE COMMERCIAL FORMULA

O ver the years, the concept of the tricolon has been incorporated into the most successful marketing messages of most multi-million-dollar brands. Below are some further examples of the basic three-word Tricolon used by some of those brands now.

Tesco – Every Little Helps

Walmart – Always Low Prices

Chrysler – Imported From Detroit

General Electric – Imagination At Work

AT&T – Mobilizing Your World

Suzuki – Way of Life

Kawasaki – Powering Your Potential

Samsung – Turn on Tomorrow

DHL – Excellence Simply Delivered

All the companies mentioned have huge advertising budgets and spend fortunes commissioning advertising agencies to come up with memorable and effective slogans. It speaks volumes that time after time they come back to the ultra-reliable Tricolon formula.

And this is where you can learn from the big boys and girls. You do not have to spend fortunes on advertising and marketing agencies to achieve equally effective results in your own work.

As Isaac Newton once said, "I have seen further by standing on the shoulders of giants". This is what you must do.

Just duplicate the techniques you have learned here. Use them in your emails, social media posts and other communications and achieve equally amazing results. Don't overdo it, but learn to use the techniques wisely, deliberately, and strategically just like Caesar, Shakespeare, Dickens, Trump, Obama, Tesco, MacDonald's and all the rest. If it works for them, it will work for you!

I read recently about a cruise ship that got into problems due to an infection onboard. So, to avoid any more infections, all those onboard were asked to wash their hands as regularly as possible to minimize the chances of the infection spreading. To address this, the captain of the ship added a tricolon (wash your hands, wash your hands, wash your hands) at the end of his daily announcement. Repeating something three times is always a good way of emphasizing a point to make people remember it.

A couple of similar examples of that technique are **Location, Location, Location** which was used to emphasize the most important factor for consideration when buying real estate. And then there was **Education, Education, Education** used by politician Tony Blair in 2003 when he wished to give prominence to his number one political priority at the time.

Due to the Tricolon's ability to be seared into the memory of the target audience, it has been used heavily and to great effect during the Covid-19 pandemic. In the UK the slogan **Hands, Face, Space** was used to hammer home the message

Hands, Face, Space

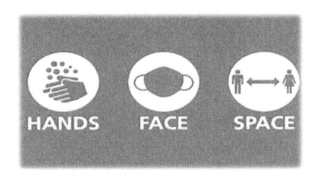

And on another occasion the lectern of the UK Prime Minister Boris Johnson was the slogan

'Stay Alert, Control the Virus, Save Lives'

In the 16th Century William Shakespeare famously used the Tricolon "Friends, Romans, Countrymen" in his play Julius Caesar which was first performed in 1599. In the 19th Century Jane Austen used the Tricolon formula with Sense and Sensibility and Pride and Prejudice. Soon after, Charles Dickens used the same formula (possibly inspired by Austen) for his titles The Pickwick Papers and A Christmas Carol.

If you are observant, you will have noticed the use of alliteration in the titles of Charles Dickens' and Jane Austen's books. And with that you have the second powerful technique applied to the title of this book. So, **the two powerful techniques applied to the title of this book are the Tricolon and Alliteration.** Ta-da! Give yourself a pat on the back if you got the correct answer.

ALLITERATION, ALLITERATION, ALLITERATION

A lliteration is simply the occurrence of the same letter or sound at the beginning of adjacent or closely connected words.

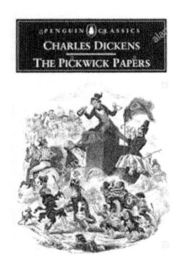

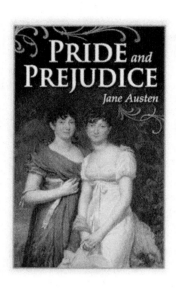

According to Wikipedia, it "is the conspicuous repetition of identical initial sounds in successive or closely associated syllables within a group of words, even those spelled differently." It is also known as head rhyme, and common examples of alliteration include "humble house", "potential power play", "picture perfect", "money matters", "rocky road", or "quick question".

Alliteration is a powerful tool that is constantly used in public speaking to persuade the audience. It is considered an "artistic constraint" which can be used by a speaker to control the audience to either feel a strong sense of urgency or maybe even an absence of urgency or whatever emotion the speaker wants to infuse into the minds of the audience.

For example, the constant repetition of P and B sounds in a speech can grab attention. Whereas, using sounds of H and E will make the audience more relaxed and less apprehensive. A constant S sound makes the audience feel like the speaker is insincere and gives them a feeling of danger. After some deep research, you will find that almost any emotion can be triggered by alliteration. Whether it is joy, peace, love, anger, hate or revenge.

Alliteration is the second powerful formula applied to the title of this book; "Power and Persuasion". This, of course, takes us back to political slogans such as Build Back Better, Strong and Stable, etc. Remember the combination of the Tricolon and Alliteration has not happened by mistake. These are carefully targeted techniques deployed to seduce attract and persuade you or whoever the target audience is. These techniques work!

To this day nobody definitively knows why we love to hear words that start with the same sound, but the fact of the matter is that we do. Alliteration just works to make a phrase or sentence stick in the mind. It makes a phrase more pleasing and memorable. This fact was not lost on William Shakespeare who, as we know, spent years at Stratford Grammar School learning the classics which included the detailed study of philosophy and rhetoric.

Take this classic sentence from Shakespeare's Anthony and Cleopatra **"The barge she sat in, like a burnished throne, burned on the water: the poop was beaten gold"**.

He was at it again in Midsummer Night's Dream with **"Whereat, with blade, with bloody blameful blade. He bravely broached his boiling bloody breast"**.

Or what about his famous poem in The Tempest, **"Full Fathom Five Thy Father Lies"**.

Now that you know the formula, you will notice it a mile away. There it is, in black and white. Alliteration combined with the mighty tricolon. A killer combo!

But Shakespeare is not the only famous author that used alliteration like it was going out of fashion. Charles Dickens used it just as widely. Take *A Christmas Carol* where he described Marley as being as "dead as a door-nail". And let's not forget two of his other titles *Nicholas Nickleby* and *The Pickwick Papers*. Alliteration and the tricolon, all strategically and deliberately deployed to seduce, attract, and persuade the target audience.

Alliteration is constantly being used by politicians and marketers to make attention grabbing and memorable messages.

In John F. Kennedy's inaugural address, he used this rhetorical device 21 times. Here is a short section of that speech.

"Finally, whether you are CITIZENS of America or CITIZENS of the world, ask of us here the **SAME high STANDARDS of STRENGTH and SACRIFICE** which we ask of you. With a good conscience our only sure reward, with history the final judge of our deeds, let us go forth to **LEAD the LAND we LOVE**, asking His blessing and His help, but knowing that here on Earth God's work must truly be our own." — John F. Kennedy.

Here are other examples of where alliteration was used in speeches:

"We, the people, declare today that the most evident of truths—that all of us are created equal—is the star that guides us still; just as it guided our forebears through **Seneca Falls,** and **Selma, and Stonewall**; just as it guided all those men and women, sung and unsung, who left footprints along this great Mall, to hear a preacher say that we cannot walk alone; to hear a King proclaim that our individual freedom is inextricably bound to the freedom of every soul on Earth". — Barack Obama.

"And our nation itself is testimony to the love our veterans have had for it and for us. All for which America stands is safe today because brave men and women have been ready to **face the fire at freedom's front."** — Ronald Reagan, Vietnam Veterans Memorial Address.

"**Four** score and seven years ago our **fathers brought forth** on this continent a new nation, conceived in liberty, and dedicated to the proposition that all men are created equal". — Abraham Lincoln, Gettysburg Address.

POWER OF THREE

I think we've proven beyond all reasonable doubt that the tricolon is one of the most powerful rhetorical formulas known to man, but even if you beg to differ, the examples you have seen cannot lie; from multibillion dollar brands to presidents and famous leaders to William Shakespeare himself. They all utilize the power of the mighty Tricolon.

Simply put, there is something commanding about the number three. Roy Peter Clark also agrees with this as he writes in his book (Writing Tools: 50 Essential Strategies for Every Writer) and I quote; "[T]hree provides a sense of the whole ... the number three is greater than four. The mojo of three offers a greater sense of completeness than four or more. ... Use one for power. Two for comparison, contrast. Three for completeness, wholeness, roundness ..."

A common example of the power of three is the story of a world champion of public speaking, Craig Valentine, who used the rule of three to make his educational presentations much more effective than his presentation skills could make them. He applied the rule of three to his workshop, 7 secrets to speaking success, and converted the seven-point lecture into a three-point lecture. What happened afterward was remarkable. There was a record level of attention from the audience, and they were better able to organize the points they received from the lecture and even remember more from what they learned from him.

In 2014, an article by Suzanne B. Shu and Kurt A, Carlson was published in the Journal of Marketing titled **"When Three Charms but Four Alarms**: Identifying the Optimal Number of Claims in Persuasion Settings" that shared research on how people react to persuasion messages.

In one of the studies, a persuasive message was created for a breakfast cereal. The results made it super clear that using one or two claims about why a person should buy the cereal was good but using three claims worked better. It was found to be more persuasive and got more people to buy the product than two claims.

But guess what happened when they used four claims? If you guessed that it performed better, you are wrong. What happened was the opposite of what anyone would naturally expect. Instead of the prospective buyers being impressed by a product that had four claims, they were suddenly overcome by skepticism and doubted the claims being made. When they were presented with four claims, they doubted all the claims.

When the message on the cereal package read; **"healthier, better tasting, and with higher quality ingredients,"** the prospects were impressed with the product and the messaging. But when it was improved to; "healthier, better tasting, crunchier, and with higher quality ingredients," the participants of the study began to perceive the cereal brand as phony or fake and that they (the cereal company) were only out to make money rather than truly inform the consumer about what the product could really do.

This experiment was carried out for different products on different fields and industries and as you might have guessed, the results were the same. One was good, two was better, **three was the best,** and when they pushed it to four, the conversion went super low.

The legendary Steve Jobs used the rule of three in the creation of Apple. Somehow, he was able to frame the idea of the **Apple iPhone** as a product with three distinct products **(an iPod, a phone, and an Internet device).** This was part of what made the Apple product so phenomenal and why it remains on top of the market. Although the initial offers are no longer pronounced, the marketing of the Apple Company continues to follow in that path of the rule of three.

And last but not least, if you're still skeptical about how much we love the power three, let's take a walk down memory lane to wartime Britain with Winston Churchill and his famous Blood, Sweat and Tears speech. At least that's how people remember it! In his speech to the House of Commons on 13th May 1940 what he actually said was, 'Blood, Toil, Tears and Sweat'. But such is our love for the Tricolon formula that most people today remember it as 'Blood, Sweat and Tears'.

THE CONSPIRACY THEORY

Adolf Hitler - "What luck for rulers that men do not think."

A s I researched for the content of this book, I soon began to wonder why such a simple and effective persuasive formula was not taught in more detail in mainstream schooling. I could see it was more widely used today than ever before and particularly by those in power and advertising. Why is it largely only taught to those receiving a privileged (private) education?

Here's where it gets controversial.

My honest and true belief is that the privileged few who know when and how to use the Tricolon formula keep it to themselves because they fear if the wider population understood its power, they would become much more difficult to control and manipulate.

One analogy you might draw is of the privileged few in society being similar to members of a Magic circle, who only share details of their craft amongst members of their own fraternity.

By doing so they ensure their secrets stay safe and they are able maintain their ability to deceive their target audience.

If you want to learn about the Tricolon in any detail (and any other of more than 30 ancient rhetorical devices) then arguably the best areas to study are Politics, Philosophy, and Economics which is better known in political circles as P.P.E.

The philosophy element is particularly important because that is where you find the study of rhetoric and the ancient rhetorical devices including the mighty Tricolon.

If you really want to up your chances of gaining high political office, studying PPE at Oxford or Cambridge in the U.K will be of great benefit. If you live in the United States, just head for Harvard or Yale.

In the U.K., Oxford and Cambridge Universities have produced most of the Prime Ministers' Cabinet Ministers, Senior Politicians, Judges, and influential voices in the media. Robert Peel, William Gladstone, Clement Atlee, Anthony Eden, Harold Macmillan, Alec Douglas-Home, Harold Wilson, Edward Heath, Margaret Thatcher, Tony Blair, David Cameron and Theresa May all attended Oxford or Cambridge Universities.

In the Unites States, Harvard and Yale Universities have produced the highest number of American Presidents. Theodore

Roosevelt, Franklin D Roosevelt, John F Kennedy, Gerald Ford, George W Bush, Barak Obama, and Bill Clinton.

You may have heard of a gentleman called Rupert Murdoch, but for those who haven't, he's the most powerful media mogul of the 21st Century. He's a billionaire businessman who owns hundreds of local, national, and international publishing outlets around the world. In the U.K he owns The Times and The Sun newspapers. In the United States he owns The Wall Street Journal and The New York Post. He is also Chairman of The Fox Corporation which owns Fox News. And no prizes for guessing.........he studied Politics, Philosophy and Economics (PPE) at Oxford University.

Since persuasive rhetorical techniques were developed two and a half thousand years ago the upper and ruling classes have fully understood that to control and influence the mass population, they must control the language. To this day and they continue to ensure that they do just that.

Most leaders are not physically stronger than their opponents. However, they must be proficient at controlling the language, above all else. Take Franklin D. Roosevelt for example. Paralyzed in 1921, he lacked all the physical strength and agility of his opponents, but he made up for it with his impressive use of words. He was regarded as a great orator, and through his persuasive skills, he rose to become the 32nd President of the most powerful nation in the world at that time.

This book may not be too popular with those in positions of power and influence, but I hope you have enjoyed this quick insight into one of the best kept secrets of the privileged few. As a result of reading this book, you are now far better equipped than the vast majority of the population and will be able to see through any attempt to seduce, attract and sometimes manipulate you.

I hope you enjoyed this book and that it was real insight into something you weren't previously aware of, but all good things must come to an end. That said, I'd love to hear your thoughts on this book and the mighty Tricolon. Do you have a favourite Tricolon? Have you seen any good ones in your travels that you'd like to share with me? I saw a classic recently. It was the name above a baby clothing shop, 'Bonny Baby Bouncer', which I thought was an excellent use of the Tricolon/Alliteration formula. It certainly stuck in my mind! So, I'd love to hear your thoughts. You can do that by contacting me on Instagram at #PowerandPersuasion.

Printed in Great Britain
by Amazon